By December 1776, the American colonists had been at war for a year against the mother country, England. The Revolution had gone badly. Now an attack by the daring American commander in chief, George Washington, might turn the tide. The Battle of Trenton began on Christmas night.

This presentation of the Battle of Trenton is unparalleled in books for young readers. Panoramic views of battlefields, close glimpses of officers and men, details of encounters are portrayed through photographs of dioramas — scale models — meticulously faithful to history in every detail.

Mark Duggan is a student of military history, particularly of the American Revolutionary War period. He is an editor and rewrite man, working on books for young people as well as for adults. He lives in New York.

The editors wish to thank David Lewis and the American Liberties Foundation, Washington Crossing, Pennsylvania, for permission to photograph the Washington Crossing Historama; the Military Miniatures Collectors Society, Boston, Massachusetts; the following collectors, whose miniatures appear: Thomas Lyman, Robert Forget, Gardiner H. Marchant, Jr., Henri Lion, John Hurley, Judson Pratt, Hicks Atwell, John Bojar; the Miniature Tactics Society, Long Island, New York, especially Harold Craig and John Blake; The Old Barracks Association, Trenton, New Jersey; Lt. Col. Vorin E. Whan, Assistant Professor of Military Art and Engineering, the United States Military Academy, West Point, New York, for his expert assistance with text and pictures.

GREAT
BATTLES OF
HISTORY

TRENTON

Mark Duggan, author
Irv Dolin, photographer
Lt. Col. Vorin E. Whan, military consultant

A Holly Book

THE WORLD PUBLISHING COMPANY
Cleveland and New York

Prepared by Specialized Publishing in conjunction with The World Publishing Company • Published by The World Publishing
Company • 2231 West 110th Street, Cleveland, Ohio 44102 • Published simultaneously in Canada by Nelson, Foster &
Scott Ltd. • Copyright © 1966 by Specialized Publishing • All rights reserved • No part of this book may be reproduced in
any form without written permission from the publisher, except for brief passages included in a review appearing in a
newspaper or magazine • Library of Congress Catalog Card Number: 66-15990 • Printed in the United States of America

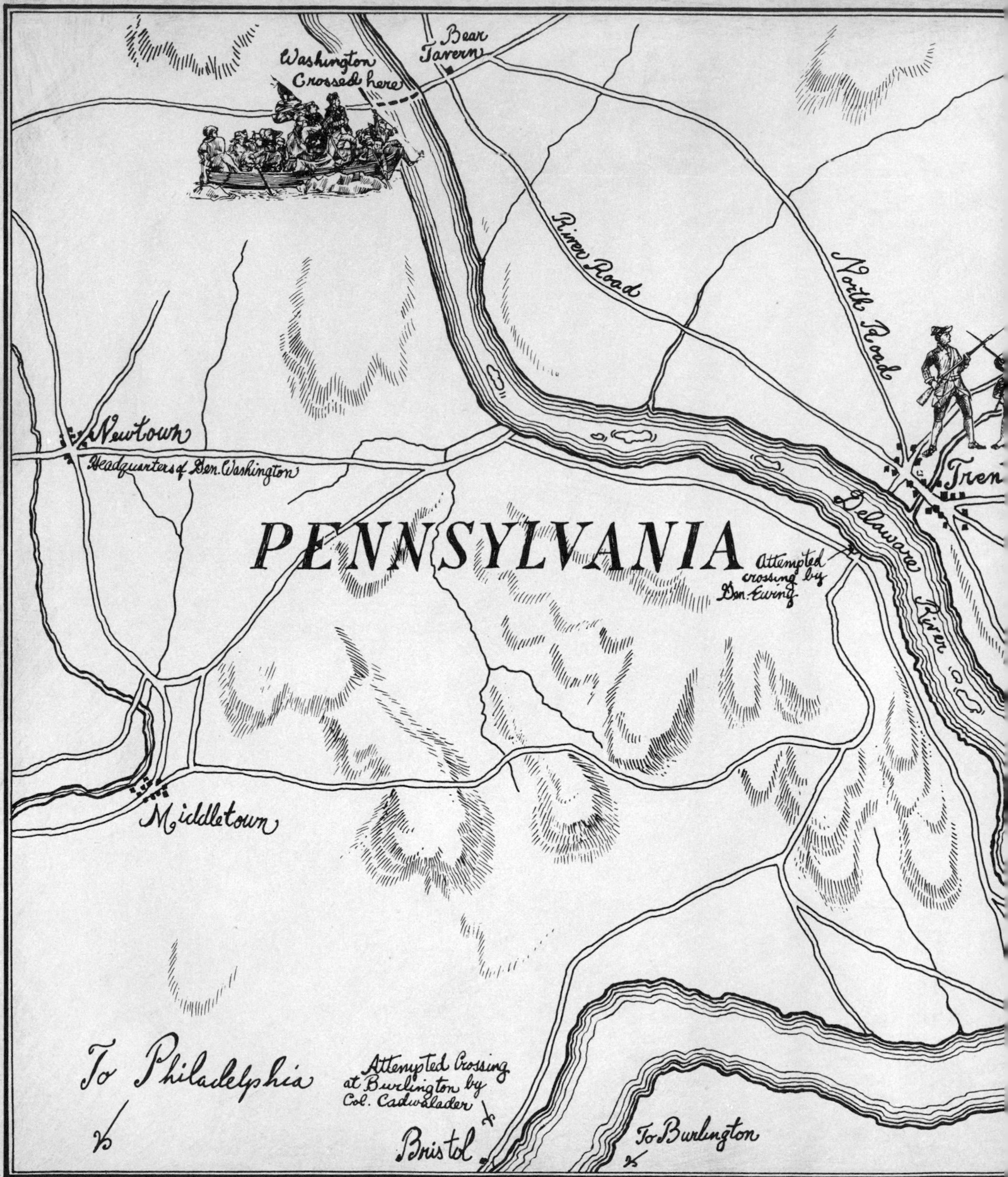

Washington
Crossed here

Bear
Tavern

River Road

North Road

Newtown
Headquarters of Gen. Washington

PENNSYLVANIA
Attempted crossing by Gen. Ewing.

Delaware River

Trenton

Middletown

To Philadelphia

Attempted Crossing at Burlington by Col. Cadwalader

Bristol

To Burlington

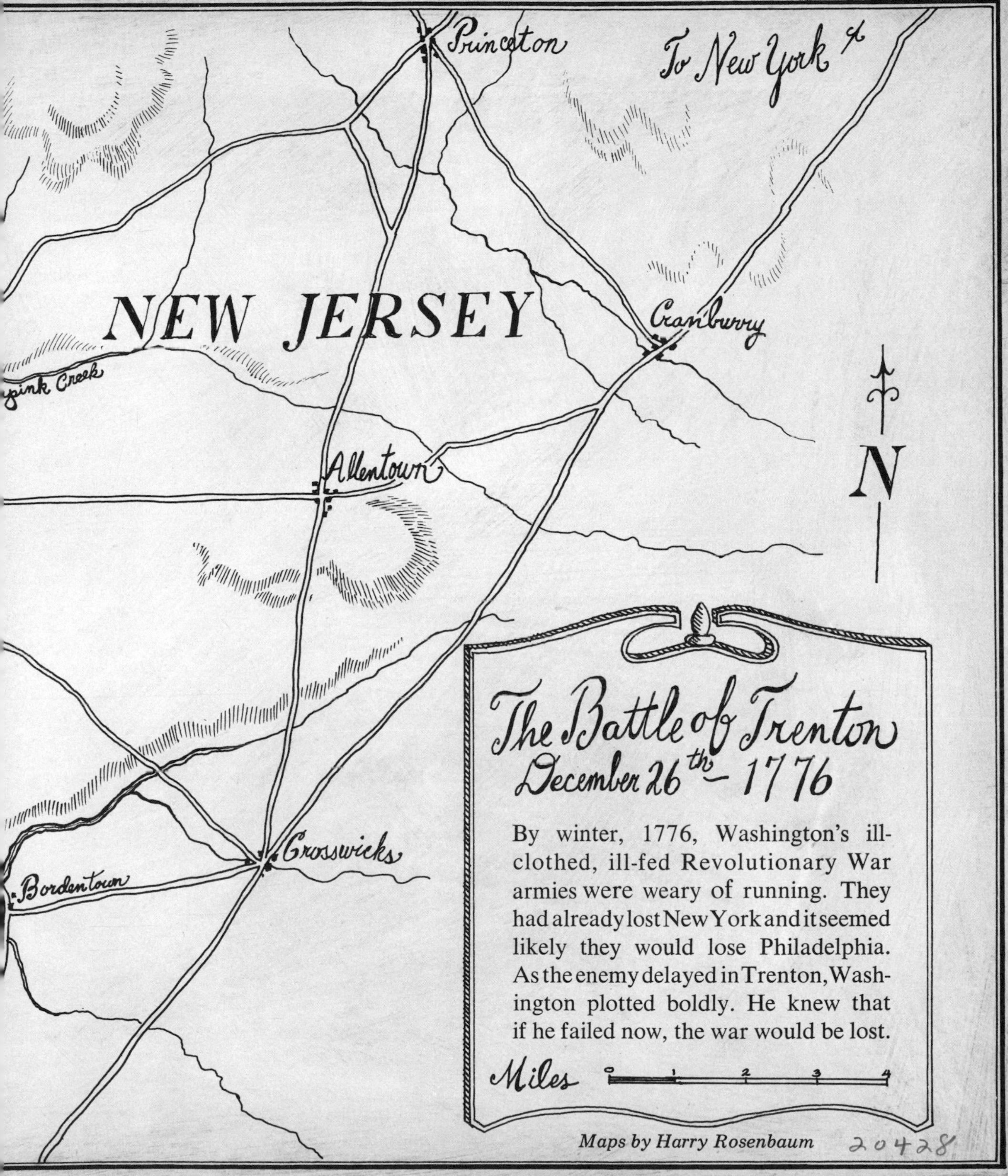

Princeton

To New York ✛

NEW JERSEY

Cranbury

ssink Creek

Allentown

N

The Battle of Trenton
December 26th – 1776

By winter, 1776, Washington's ill-clothed, ill-fed Revolutionary War armies were weary of running. They had already lost New York and it seemed likely they would lose Philadelphia. As the enemy delayed in Trenton, Washington plotted boldly. He knew that if he failed now, the war would be lost.

Crosswicks

Bordentown

Miles 0   1   2   3   4

Maps by Harry Rosenbaum

20428

The Game Was Nearly Up

In ragged coat, shoes worn thin, an American sentry watches through the raw, damp night.

It was December of 1776, the second year of the American Revolution, and one word summed u the story of the past year for the patriots—retreat.

General George Washington, the commander of the Continental army. saw a chance to turn the tide—an attack on the unsuspecting, enemy-hel town of Trenton, New Jersey, sitting on the far side of the Delaware Rive like a fat hen before a hungry fox.

The risk was enormous, and defea would be final. But the time had come to stand and fight. The enemy' guard was down. The British though they had the Continentals beaten.

And they very nearly did. Genera Washington's army was desperate. His men were huddled around their winter campfires, baking pasty cake of flour and water, shivering in their torn and threadbare uniforms. Some were barefoot. It was as ragtag, bobtail an army as war had ever see

But these were the faithful soldier who had not deserted, and they still had heart for battle. With this little army Washington was determined to march on Trenton. And to take it.

*George Washington,
the Continental army
commander in chief.*

Some are without shoes, some without guns that fire; there are no summer patriots in Washington's army.

A British fife and drum corps (top) celebrates the arrival of troops from England. They have come to show the upstart colonists the error of their ways, but the rebels (below) have other plans for the interfering English.

The cause of liberty was at stake. The year before, the American colonies had declared themselves independent of their mother country, England. The king and all the king's men must leave them free, they had said. For, in this new nation of "united states," men were born equal with the right to govern themselves.

England's army had leapt to the challenge. Ten thousand strong, it had met the rebels with musket, sword, and cannon. At Concord and Lexington, two quiet Massachusetts towns, the first shots had been fired, and the Revolutionary War had begun.

Months later, in Boston, the full British military force had charged the stubborn rebels, who were entrenched on Bunker Hill. Whole lines of redcoats had dropped before the rebel muskets. And the brave defenders had not yielded until their ammunition had given out.

From all the colonies, men had flocked to join the fight for freedom. They had even besieged the British in their stronghold of Boston. And here the Americans won their only complete victory of the war.

In April, 1775, Americans, determined to take no more abuse, turn the British back at Concord Bridge.

War begins on Lexington Green, where both British and patriot blood is shed.

11

Better farmers than soldiers, brave patriots dig in and battle fiercely for their independence.

With a superhuman effort, the rebels broke the British hold on Boston.

Cannon were needed to drive the enemy out. But the only cannon the rebels owned were hundreds of miles away, deep in the forests of New York at Fort Ticonderoga.

One morning, the British in Boston awakened to find those guns leveled at them from the heights above the city. Men and horses hauled the cannon over rough terrain, frozen rivers, and snow-locked mountains to Boston. Before those cannon, the British fled.

The Americans next fought on Long Island, and on Manhattan island. And the grim pattern of retreat took shape.

Now it was winter again. Pressed by the British army, the Continental fell back beyond the Delaware River, to Newtown, Pennsylvania.

"The game," thought Washington, "is pretty near up." Thousands of men deserted or fell ill. And even the few dollars a month pay they were supposed to draw had dwindled. And on January 1, most of the men could head for home, their terms of

By entrenching in secret on Dorchester Heights, Americans force British troops to evacuate Boston.

enlistment completed. The new nation would find itself without an army.

General Washington might go on retreating. But he would go with only a remnant of the Revolutionary army. How many fighting men could be expected to endure—year after year—the hardships and the humiliation of defeat?

Who could argue with those who said the British had won the war?

Bloodied and weakened from the Battle of Long Island, the Americans retreat.

Hessians led by Colonel Johann Rall occupy Trenton, most strategic point in the British line of defense.

The chimneys of about a hundred houses smoked cosily in Trenton that December of 1776. Their small rooms bulged with broad-shouldered men in uniform who spoke and joked in a language strange to the ears of the New Jerseyans.

These were the newly arrived Hessian mercenaries, soldiers hired in Europe by the British to help put down the rebellion. Fighting was their business. They did it for pay and they did it well. These were the same soldiers who had stormed the heights of Fort Washington, on the Hudson River, pulling themselves up the cliffs by the roots of trees in the face of rebel musketry.

Three regiments of Hessian soldiers were now in Trenton, under the command of Colonel Johann Rall. The colonel had fought with great courage at Fort Washington and, flushed with victory, he had demanded a winter headquarters of his own. The English gave him the command of Trenton, the strategic spot along their line of defense, just across the river from the camp of the Continental army.

16

Colonel Rall likes garrison life to be colorful. Every morning he gives orders for a full-dress parade.

To the Hessians fighting is a trade. They do it for pay, and officers like this one make sure they do it well.

New Jerseyans, once loyal to the British, grow tired of the way Hessian soldiers abuse them.

Colonel Rall was pleased with his neat and prosperous town. He would lead a rather princely life this winter. And in the spring he would capture Philadelphia, just a few miles away.

At Rall's side as he rode into Trenton was his commander, Colonel Carl von Donop, an officer wise in the ways of many wars. Von Donop's practiced eye scanned the town as a potential battle site while Colonel Rall was house hunting, looking for a headquarters. Rall would find his house either on King Street or on Queen Street. These were Trenton's two thoroughfares, running down to the Delaware like the sides of a blunted wedge pointing north toward Princeton.

"Well, Colonel Rall, you will want to get your fortifications up as soon as possible," von Donop said. "Your points of weakness are the ferry here and the intersection to the north. If you like, I'll send my engineer tomorrow to look the place over."

Rall smiled. "I hardly think we will have need, Colonel. That army of farmers has been on the run for a solid month."

18

For food and furniture, the Hessians plunder colonial homes, ignoring the pleas and protests of owners.

A British soldier assigned to Rall's forces draws fresh drinking water from a nearby stream.

Hessian troops grow increasingly uneasy when Rall fails to fortify their position at Trenton.

So the Hessian occupation of Trenton quickly settled into routine. Picket stations were set up on all roads leading into town. Soldiers were quartered in almost every building, even in the church. For his own headquarters, Colonel Rall had chosen a comfortable house which overlooked the churchyard on King Street.

Colonel Rall liked garrison life to be colorful. Every morning a full parade was held for the changing of the guard, with musicians in the lead, gleaming cannon hitched to horses, every bayonet, boot, and uniform button polished to perfection.

But the defense of Trenton was neglected. Von Donop's engineer did, in fact, lay plans for two fortifications. One was to be at the junction of King and Queen Streets. The second was to be an entrenchment at the ferry landing. Yet, on Rall's orders, work had gone no farther than gathering wood.

Colonel Rall was pleased with his parades, but his officers grew uneasy. Their lines of communication were cut by outriders from Washington's camp. Spies came and went as they

pleased, and there were rumors that
General Washington was planning
a move, incredible as that might seem.

Nor was the Trenton population
happy. Once loyal to the king, it was
turning against the British and the
Hessian soldiers, who were plundering
homes—taking anything that could
be picked up and carried off.

The security of Colonel Rall's
garrison crumbled. It was gradually
turning into a nervous and harried
outpost. Even Rall grew uneasy.
Perhaps he should have
reinforcements. On a biting cold day,
he dispatched this suggestion to his
general. The courier returned with
the insulting reply:

"Tell the colonel he is safe. I will
keep the peace with a corporal's
guard if necessary."

Rall was boiling with anger when
Major von Dechow, commander of
one of the regiments, came to request
that work on the fortifications be
resumed as protection against possible
rebel attack.

Rall's answer: "Let them come,
Major. We have bayonets. What do
we want with trenches?"

*At the ferry landing, entrenching work goes no
further than having some soldiers gather wood.*

21

Victory or Death

John Honeyman (above), a local cattle dealer, provides General Washington with important information to help his ragtag Continentals (below) defeat the Hessian troops at Trenton.

General Washington had prepared carefully. Part of his preparation was gathering secret information from paid spies.

One of his most daring informants was one John Honeyman, a New Jersey cattle dealer, on whom the Hessians depended for supplies.

As the cattle dealer was going about his business on a farm near Trenton one afternoon, a roving band of Continentals on horseback pounded down the frozen lane, jumped the fence, and rode John Honeyman down. Tied with his own rope, he found himself being ferried across the Delaware.

Acting the part of an angry prisoner, Honeyman was brought to General Washington for questioning. It was nearly an hour before the prisoner left the general and was marched to the guardhouse.

Honeyman had done his job well. While he had been with the American leader, he had revealed all he knew about the Hessians in Trenton. All that remained was for Honeyman to escape so that he could return across the river.

Washington has many spies like Honeyman and makes certain they are treated well for their work.

That night, a haystack caught fire. In the confusion, the prisoner heard the lock on his door spring back. Quickly he let himself out, dodged a sentry, and was off.

Back in Trenton, he delivered to Colonel Rall the news that the Continental army could not possibly mount an attack. It was, he reported, too nearly paralyzed from cold and hunger to be a threat.

Rebels near Trenton find sport in harassing Hessian outposts.

Washington orders his weary army to gather at McKonkey's Ferry. He plans a massive attack.

The time had come to strike the blow. The cause of liberty could no longer be kept alive simply by evading the British.

How many men did the Continental army have fit for duty? Four thousand, Washington was told—two thousand less than he had hoped.

"No matter, gentlemen. I am resolved to take Trenton," he said.

The battle plan was formed. The attack on Trenton would be three-pronged. Washington, with more than two thousand men, under the immediate command of General Nathanael Greene, would cross the river at McKonkey's Ferry, eight miles upstream. Directly opposite Trenton, a force of six hundred, under General James Ewing, would cross to the ferry landing to cut off any retreat to the south.

A thousand men under Colonel John Cadwalader would cross down river to block any reinforcements sent up from the south. All the crossings would be made in the darkness of Christmas night. The attack itself would be made one hour before dawn, December 26.

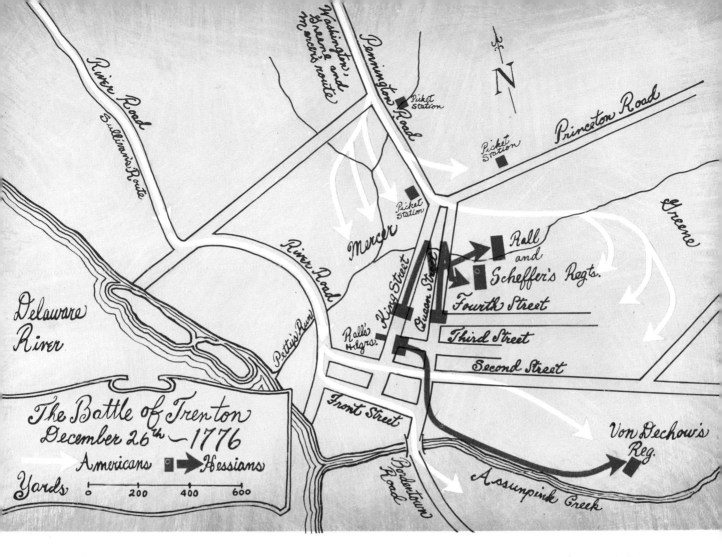

The Battle of Trenton
December 26th — 1776

→ Americans ■→ Hessians

Yards
0   200   400   600

Washington's main force would march down on Trenton from its landing eight miles north. It would split into two columns. One would enter Trenton at the north, by Pennington Road. The other, under General John Sullivan, would enter by the river road. It would be an onrushing attack, to take the enemy by surprise.

27

A drummer boy, all spit and polish, plays a bright tattoo.

Continental cannon is dragged to the ferry crossing, in preparation for the coming battle.

Marbleheaders, Washington's sea-going men, will ferry his troops across the frigid Delaware.

A crucial part of the attack plan was the tremendous job of ferrying men, horses, and cannon across the river. The key to success would be in the hands of the sea-going soldiers from the port of Marblehead, Massachusetts.

"Colonel Glover," Washington said to the leader of the Marbleheaders, "you and your men did it at Brooklyn Heights. Can you do it again?" The weathered face of the soldier showed a faint glow of pride.

"We will do it, sir."

Colonel Glover's men were in their element on the frigid waters of the Delaware, gathering all the boats they could find and tying them up in readiness. The great black boats, called Durhams, were some forty feet long and could be steered from either end. Not even the horses and the heavy artillery were too much for them.

In the cold, thin sunlight of mid-afternoon, December 24, General Washington and his aide, Colonel Baylor, with an escort of six light-horse troopers, rode to a house outside of Newtown, Pennsylvania.

Every Continental, from rifleman to cannoneer, helps to make ready for the planned assault.

Alone and in pairs, the officers arrived to meet in private with their commander in chief. Grace was said, the meal begun, and the plan of battle reviewed. The rugged John Stark leaned forward.

"General, if I may say it, if you expect to establish the independence of these states, you must teach your men to place dependence upon firearms and courage."

Stark was voicing Washington's thoughts. Those lessons in courage would certainly be learned in the next hours. There were no trenches in Trenton. Their objective could be taken only by onslaught of cannon shot, rifle fire, and bayonets.

These are brave men Washington leads. They are tired of running and glad for the fight ahead.

29

Washington's Bold Decision

In dead of night, Colonel Henry Knox, a hero many times over, orders his guns into the boats.

A fast-falling snow and biting wind fail to deter the gathering forces. They move swiftly ahead.

On Christmas day, 1776, the Continental soldiers were pleased. There was a fight just ahead, and the had sickened of running and waiting. Their blood was up for battle as the readied their muskets.

The brigades lined up and began their march. Orders were harsh: "A profound silence to be enjoine and no man to quit the ranks on pain of death." Two guides went with each brigade, and all the officer placed white ribbons on their hats so their men would know them in the darkness.

By sundown all were on the move including Colonel Henry Knox's cannon and howitzers. Beside one gun marched a slight figure, his tricorn hat pulled down low over his brow. This was Alexander Hamilton an eighteen-year-old captain, whose unit of New York artillery was one of the best disciplined in the army.

There was no power on earth that could do anything about the weather A fast-falling snow and biting wind cut the marching men to the bone an turned the road from Newtown into test of endurance for men and horse

32

Into the great Durham boats the American troops go—and then out into the treacherous ice-jammed river.

While the Continental army was struggling toward its objective, the Hessians in Trenton were making the best of a Christmas away from home. There was beer enough to go around, warm fires, and the company of the women who had followed them from New York. Except for the snow that began to fall, it seemed as good a Christmas as any army at the front might hope for.

Raw winds bite the face and chill the bones as the boats push slowly onward.

33

They cross in silence, to the rhythm of wind and water and the ice floes striking the boats.

That night, Colonel Rall went to a festive party at the home of Abraham Hunt, a wealthy resident of Trenton. The house was hung with fragrant pine and holly. There was good food, fine Madeira wine, warm candlelight, and—most to the colonel's taste—a well-played card game.

The hour grew late. A servant opened the front door of the Hunt home to the desperate knock of a Loyalist farmer begging to see Colonel Rall. The servant did his duty and kept the man out, but agreed to take his note to the Hessian colonel.

Perhaps Rall at that moment faced a ticklish turn of his cards. When the note was handed to him, he stuffed it in his pocket without reading it. On the slip of paper, the farmer had written that Washington's army was crossing the Delaware.

It was true. The force under Washington was getting across the treacherous river. Colonel Knox was standing at the shore, giving out the orders of embarkation in his deep voice. The waters of the river were swift and full of floating ice that ground against the boats. Gun

34

carriages rumbled, horses whinnied and resisted, men cursed, but the snow and wind were unrelenting.

Each brigade knew its place and when to step forward into the great black boats. From among the first men to reach the New Jersey side, sentinels were posted around the landing place. The watchword for that night was "Victory or Death."

One by one, the brigades were ferried to the Jersey shore. It was 3 A.M. when all had safely crossed the river. Eight miles of road still lay between them and Trenton. It would be full daylight before the men could cover that distance. Their chance for a surprise attack might well be lost.

Throughout the night, General Washington saw the odds against success mounting. From Colonel Cadwalader to the south came the news that a crossing there was hopeless, for the ice swirling down the river was jamming in jagged piles that reached almost from shore to shore. Ewing's six hundred men directly opposite Trenton were in the same fix. The battle depended on the main force alone.

Horses whinny in answer to raging winds, and too often grow restless and hard to control.

As each boat empties, it returns for more men. Thousands must cross the Delaware this night.

By 3 A.M., the Americans are safely across—but a long, cold march to Trenton lies ahead.

There was another serious misfortune. The snow that was coming down now was mixed with rain and had rendered some of the men's muskets useless by wetting the priming powder in the firing pans. If the troops had not had bayonets at the ends of those guns, General Washington might have turned back.

There was one small thing to be thankful for: the wind was at the men's backs as they covered the slippery miles. Washington rode along the column, muffled in his cloak.

"Press on, boys," he urged, "press on. Keep close to your officers."

After about a mile on the march, at the Bear Tavern, the column divided into right and left wings. General John Sullivan led his brigade off toward the river approach to the town, while Washington and Greene pressed on by the north road.

Halfway to their objective, at about the hour Washington had earlier hoped to start his attack, a brief halt was called. Exhausted men drew breakfast rations from their packs, and many lay down on the snowy ground to sleep. Soon the weary men were marching once more.

Three miles from Trenton, a group of some forty Continentals came to meet the marchers in the spreading gray dawn. This was a company that had been sent ahead earlier to take prisoner anyone going into or coming out of Trenton. It had been a quiet watch. The night before, the men of the Trenton garrison had gone heavily to bed, brimful of beer. Not even a patrol had been out that morning.

Whatever the odds, Washington was determined to go ahead with the attack. Even the dauntless Sullivan was having misgivings about doing battle with so many useless muskets. To General Sullivan's messenger, Washington said:

"Tell the general to use the bayonet and penetrate the town, for the town must be taken, and I am resolved to take it."

At any moment, Trenton's outlying picket stations would break into sight. All men readied their bayonets.

While all of Trenton slept, the Continentals were coming at it on the run, and "all were fierce for battle."

The Continental Army was coming toward Trenton on the run. All were "fierce for battle."

Washington warms himself by a fire and waits as his army prepares to move on.

37

Surprise
at Trenton

Bold Continentals, their feet bloody, their weapons frozen, reach Trenton unchallenged.

At dawn the American troops surprise an enemy outpost, forcing its defenders back to Trenton.

It was 4 A.M. The usual Hessian procedure called for an early-morning patrol, equipped with two brass field pieces, to go down to the river near the Trenton ferry landing.

On this morning, December 26, Lieutenant Jacob Piel, Rall's adjutant sent the two artillerymen on to Major von Dechow. The men trudged to the major's quarters through deep snow.

Major von Dechow considered for a fateful moment. Was it worth sending the men out in such vile weather? He made his decision. The men need not make the patrol.

What the patrol would have seen and heard if it had gone to the ferry landing were the persistent efforts of Ewing and his men to get across the Delaware. Von Dechow's decision was to prove a fatal error.

Another Hessian patrol turned back too soon that morning. If the men of the river road picket station had patrolled their usual four miles up the road, they might well have run into General Sullivan's advancing column. But on this morning only three men went out, and they contented themselves with going a very short distance. Washington's army neared Trenton unchallenged.

The first man to see the enemy was the lieutenant in charge of the Pennington Road picket station. When he saw the incredible sight, he shouted frantically to his men, "Der Feind! Der Feind!" (The enemy!)

Faced by the attackers, the Hessians had time only to grab their guns and run for town.

"We entered the town with them pell-mell," wrote Colonel Knox later to his wife, "and there succeeded a scene of war which I have often conceived, but never saw before."

As the picket stations on the north road were being forced by Greene's men, Hessian pickets on the river road were meeting the wrathful Sullivan. Caught between advancing Continentals, they retreated east to the town.

At the first sound of gunfire from the picket stations, Lieutenant Piel ran from his quarters and quickly sounded the alarm.

Colonel Rall roused himself from sleep and came to his window to ask, "What is the matter?"

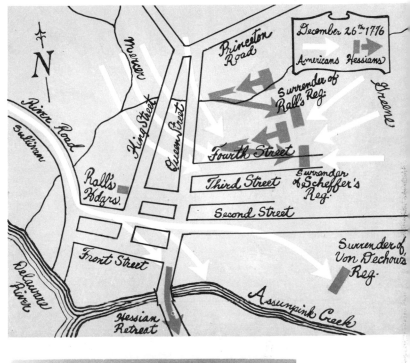

One Hessian falls wounded; his comrades take time only to seize their arms and run for town.

41

Hessian defenders at the barracks, lining up in neat rows, become easy marks for the attackers.

Piel spread the alarm further. A lieutenant turned out the troops quartered in the church, then dashe to rouse Lieutenant Colonel Francis Scheffer, commander of one of the three Hessian regiments. Scheffer, who had been sick in bed, dragged himself out and sent the lieutenant ask Colonel Rall where his men should form.

Rall was dressed by now and in the fray. Scheffer's regiment, he decided, should form behind the church. About one-half the men of Rall's own regiment were ready for action, under the command of Lieutenant Colonel Balthasar. They advanced north on King Street.

As Rall was mounting his excited horse, the enormity of the situation began to dawn on him.

"My God, Lieutenant Englehardt he shouted at an artillery officer, "the pickets are already coming in. Push your cannon ahead." But the Continental riflemen had taken cove in the houses, dried the priming pans of their muskets, and opened u a devastating fire. The cannon, too, were now in action.

As Lieutenant Colonel Brethauer led his men up King Street, they came under musket fire from Continentals on their left and at their front. Lieutenant Johann Englehardt advanced his guns in the face of cannon shot from Alexander Hamilton's artillery, already set up at the strategic and unfortified head of King Street. Englehardt got his guns into action and kept them going while men fell all around him. Among the Continentals in the line of Englehardt's fire were Captain William Washington and Lieutenant James Monroe. Under Colonel Knox's orders, they led a charge and took the Rall cannon in hand-to-hand combat. Both men were wounded, Monroe with a frightful hole in his shoulder from a Hessian ball.

With their cannon now lost, the men of the Rall regiment fell back down King Street, while Hamilton's artillery mowed through their ranks. As Colonel Scheffer tried to lead his men out of the church alley and up King Street, they were stopped by cannon fire and thrown into disorder by the retreat of Rall's men.

Wiser Continentals take cover before opening a devastating fire on the ill-prepared enemy.

Rebel artillerymen direct their cannonade on confused Hessians trying to thwart the attack.

Rall now became aware of the musket fire from Sullivan's brigades. He was being attacked from the rear.

The Hessians retreated and reformed on the open plain east of town. This was to be Colonel Rall's finest moment. Rallying his men in battalion formation, he faced the enemy with his favorite battle cry: "All who are my grenadiers, advance!"

Halfheartedly, the Hessians pressed forward, their guns repeatedly misfiring in the wet snow. The advance petered out and Colonel Rall saw with shame that his own regiment was first to falter. Perhaps Colonel Rall, at this sight, made himself an easy target, for two musket balls tore into the side of the Hessian commander and dropped him from his saddle. His men lost all heart. They surrendered.

The battle was two-thirds won. But von Dechow's regiment was still resisting, even though the major had been badly wounded. With a captain now commanding them, the troops stubbornly kept up musket fire as they fell back along the north bank of Assunpink Creek, looking

Behind the English Church the Hessians fight and die, as Colonial troops come on.

for a place where they could ford it.

Their position was impossible and, under assault from Sullivan's men, the captain surrendered.

In the early moments of the battle, when it seemed to be going well, Washington had stationed himself with his escort at an observation point north of the town, leaving the conduct of the battle to General Greene. Here, after scarcely an hour of fighting had passed, he received the news of victory. Down on the battlefield "the patriot troops tossed their hats in the air, a great shout resounded in the village, and the battle of Trenton was closed."

For many Hessians there will be no escape. They have but two choices: surrender or die.

Hessians rushing up King Street are met by a withering blast from well-placed American guns.

The inhabitants of the houses cam[e] out from behind their smashed windows and broken walls. Many Hessians lay in the slushy streets, dead or wounded.

The Continentals had captured s[ix] pieces of artillery, forty horses, and a thousand muskets. They had take[n] almost nine hundred prisoners. One hundred of the enemy had been kill[ed] or wounded. The Continentals' own casualty list was almost too light to be believed. None killed. Only Captain Washington and Lieutenan[t] Monroe and two soldiers wounded.

Washington and Greene visited the dying Colonel Rall in his headquarters. Ever the soldier, the colonel observed the formalities of surrender and asked that his men be treated kindly. He died next day; so did von Dechow.

Washington ordered withdrawal and return to the camp at Newtow[n]. The Continentals would not be safe until the Delaware was once again between them and the British.

The citizens of Trenton gathered to see the column on its way. Ther[e] was Washington, superbly graceful the saddle; the younger officers, bursting with pride in their accomplishment; Knox's artillery and the six brass cannon he would put to good use; the Hessians, shuffling along; the Continental soldiers, looking more the part of vanquished than victors in their pitiful clothing.

The victory at Trenton did not win the war for the Americans. Ahead were five long years of bitter fighting before the final moment when the British would surrender at Yorktown.

The march back was filled with hardship for the Continental troops. Many soldiers could not be ferried over the Delaware until the following day; two exhausted foot soldiers, sleeping in the snow, froze to death.

But the battle of Trenton had raised the spirits of the people. It brought new recruits to the army and encouraged seasoned men to re-enlist. And it silenced those critics who said Washington knew only how to retreat.

The war could now be fought wholeheartedly and pressed on to its end. The spirit of '76 that blazed at Trenton would never again burn low.

A mortally wounded Colonel Rall surrenders to Washington. The Americans are victorious.